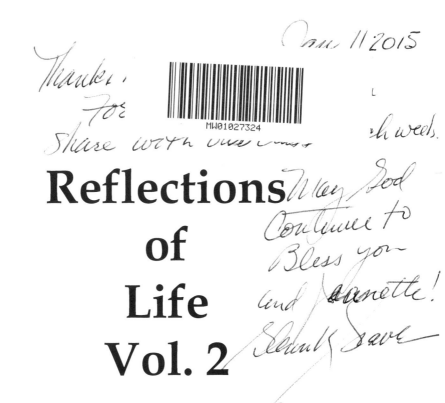

Reflections
of
Life
Vol. 2

Poetry for kids, grown-ups,
and Sunday Schools

By
Glenn Kennedy
Graves

Title: *Reflections of Life Vol. 2*

ISBN-10: 978-1500766719
ISBN-13: 1500766712

For information on ordering directly from the author, CreateSpace e-stores, amazon.com, or other sales channels, contact Glenn K. Graves at his email address: glenn@tennisglenn.com

Dedication

This collection of poetic essays, memories, and life experiences is dedicated to my son, Warren Graves, his beautiful wife, Karen, and to my three adorable grandchildren, Leela, her little brother, Deacon-River, and to their little sister, Luna.

My father, John (Jack) Atwood Graves, left me four paintings that he created in his retirement years while vacationing in Hawaii. I get to appreciate his artistic gifts every day. Since I cannot paint, or draw even a stick figure, I trust that my family will allow this collection to be my "paintings" of Life.

Author's Note

After the attack on September 11, 2001, I found that the easiest way for me to express my feelings was through poetry. The first poem, "A Call to Arms," and its follow up piece, "We Call Them Heroes," were written fifteen days later. Both of these pieces are in my first volume of poems published in 2011.

Since then, I have written about Starbucks, Tennis, Living Alone, the Real Estate Industry, Cities and Places I have been, Friendships, my son and his family, and, last but not least, my very real and personal relationship with God. I hope you enjoy these poetic interpretations of real life experiences!

Although most of the poems selected for Vol. 2 are new, I did include a few of my favorites from my first book that are needed to fill out the collection.

Glenn Kennedy Graves
October 13, 2014

Topical Contents

One for Each Month
<>
Love of Country
<>
Special Memories
<>
Grandpa's Favorites
<>
More Starbucks
<>
Animals Real and Imaginary
<>
Blessings of Christmas
<>
Essays
<>
Biblical and Christian

One
For
Each Month

January …
A New Beginning

January can be the beginning of all that is new;
Starting with a list of things you desire to do.
To Stock Brokers, for example, it's a fresh start.
Some have a business plan … some throw a dart!

January is all about goals and getting things done.
Prioritize the list, and by December you'll have won.
Set goals high and you'll have more about to shout.
Such is life; the more you put in, the more you get out!

January blooms with flowered floats on parade,
Football games and coaches drenched in Gatorade.
It goes from Times Square to a Super Bowl game.
The TV commercials are new, but the game's the same!

January is like starting over with a brand new slate;
We've done this before, but only God knows our fate!
Every year the calendar starts over again from zero.
Strive for excellence … and become your own hero!

January is a winter sunrise melting a cold, dark sky,
Slowly warming the earth, inviting birds to fly.
It encourages hope and happiness as days get longer.
It's a New Beginning … use it to become stronger!

February is a fun Month

February in San Diego can be a fun few weeks
It's that time of year when love usually peaks
And, of course, there is nothing like it in the Fall
Because it is uniquely, the shortest month of all

One Monday in February the Presidents we remember
Since George and Abe were not born in September
In years past we used to get both of these holidays
But Congress found out and didn't think it pays!

In February valentines and golf are the really big thing
But with the "Do-Not-Call" list, the phone won't ring
Checking accounts look better since taxes aren't due
And charge cards are recovering from the holidays, too.

Every four years in February, a leap-year-day we add
But for those born on the 29th don't feel quite so sad
Fortunately, they get to stay younger three years longer
And it gives your Valentine an extra day to grow fonder.

During February in San Diego, you can even see snow
And because of our mountains, to the snow we can go
Or watch the PGA Golf Tournament at Torrey Pines
For a national TV audience, San Diego really shines!

March is a Tweener!

March could probably be called a Tweener!
Since, in the Midwest the snow gets deeper
Just because the March days grow longer
Doesn't mean Winter doesn't get stronger

Colorado Aspen don't know what to think
Temperatures warm; it can snow in a blink
Spring attempts to peek out
But a hail storm can make people pout

In March, Florida oranges look great
But one last frost farmers will hate
Just when you think Winter is finally done
Cold Canadian air reminds us Nature has won

Maybe March is why Ireland has no snakes
Biting cold weather is only for Drakes
Snows start to melt and rivers start to rise
That flooding is a possibility is no surprise

But March in SoCal is a Sporting Paradise
Runners and joggers drink coffee with ice
The PGA shows off it's West Coast Swing
And March Madness is a really big thing

So whether Spring comes or Winter goes
During the month of March, who really knows
Spring will come, everybody's seen Her
And that's why March … is called a Tweener!

April Fools and Flowers

... Taxes and Life

The month of April is all about life ... refreshed and good
And I'd add a few more days to the month if I could
As the cool winds of Spring begin to warm
Robins appear on lawns and bees start to swarm

For the prankster, the 1st of April makes them drool
As they play their jokes on folks they can fool
And even though it was never my fault
I always seemed to get blamed for sugar in the salt

Yet, it's the 15th of April that is kind'a scary
The Tax Man cometh ... all wooly and hairy
For most taxpayers it is a day to get money back
While others ... borrow for the dollars they lack

April is also a great month for sport
Basketball finals explode on the court
Umpires of Baseball start to yell, "Play Ball"
And the "Masters" is in April ... not the fall

April has a reputation for colored eggs and flowers
As bulbs turn to buds from natures gentle showers
The face of the moon is still a pleasant little fellow
While the dull gray interstate tuns purple and yellow

And yet, April is perhaps the most sacred month of all
This is the month in which the Passover and Easter fall
Some people celebrate a miracle that's 2000 years new
As they take God at His word to save the lives of a few

The Wonderful Month of May

There are quite a few things to say
About the wonderful month of May
Flowers in bloom illuminate colorful hues
As the sky seems to reflect brighter blues

May has the fewest number of alphabet letters
It hosts a Derby in Kentucky with lots of betters
On one Sunday we honor Mom's with candy and lace
And celebrate Memorial Day with a famous auto race

May is kind'a like the middle month of Spring
The weather is nice; you can do just about anything
But summer is coming and gas prices will swell
And as people move about they start feeling well

Oriental countries use the first few days for fun
Imagine a lot of bright umbrellas blocking the sun
In Mexico Cinco de Mayo can really be a blast
It's really too bad, the month of May doesn't last

June Gloom

June Gloom
A SoCal phenomenon
Follows May Grey
Why do we stay?

A marine layer floats in
And stays all day.
Depressing everyone
When is it done?

The sky is dismal
Of course
People don't smile
Does it last a long while?

People from Kansas
Should go back home
Complain to your travel agent
Can you get a car to rent?

You want to stay in bed
No interest in work
Overcast, cloudy sky
Don't you just want to say, "Bye"?

You keep hoping it will go
Prayers don't work
It hides the morning sun
Does anybody have fun?

July Heat

The middle of summer
Can sometimes be a bummer!
After tolerating the gloom of June
Summer can't come too soon

And not always is July very hot
Although hot will have a shot
July can just be a prelude to heat
In which case … it can't be beat!

July is blessed with the best holiday
The 4th of July is a very festive day
Fireworks streak above the night sky
Parades and concerts are also why

Pool parties and bar-b-cues are big
Beaches are a place for kids to dig
If only you can find a parking slot
And a plot of sand to cast your lot!

July is a chance for gas prices to rise
A reason we diet for a smaller size
We head to Sea World and the Zoo
And the mountains and beaches to!

Arizonans clog our hotels and roads
As they escape the heat, snakes and toads
Our beaches attract the tourists here
Let's hope they can tolerate … laws against beer!

August Hot

August can sure be hot
It's summer … cool it's not!
Depending where you are
Hot humid air is usually not far!

August has more work days
Yet Congress still seeks delays!
But No Holidays are found
I guess more work is sound!

Gasoline prices like to climb
A lot more than just a dime !
Best to stay off the road
A Time to paint the Abode!

August is tough on a lawn
Water rates increase at drawn!
Hills turn golden brown
As Fire fighters frown!

August brings incredible heat
Causing a coastal retreat
To escape the dry and hot
Seeking any shady spot!

Baseball is in full swing
Picnics to concerts we bring
Kids at Camps have fun
Under a hot August sun!

September Sun
In San Diego

September is a hot sun
And prolongs summer fun
Congress added Labor Day
It's a lot more fun that way

Air cooled malls will fill
Dry air will linger still
Temperatures will increase
The hot will not decrease

"Zonies" will pack and go
School traffic will be slow
Shorts and sandals galore
It's cooler on the floor

Summer vacationers depart
Football seasons start
As Baseball winds down
In Ted Williams home town!

Scary and Colorful October

What a fabulous Month, is October
Temperatures drop off from September
Pumpkins and squash are at the store
Summer tries to hang on a little bit more

Neighboring La Mesa has an Octoberfest
Where a few funny folks toast all the rest
Yet, dry hills to the east appear very scary
For every firefighter this month is hairy

With no major holidays to shorten a week
Sales increase with more time to speak
Days grow shorter; leaves change colors and fall
TV is overrun by a World Series and football

And just when October gets ready to leave
Goblins show up with a trick up their sleeve
Some costumes worn can be rather shocking
But kids enjoy … going door to door knocking

A lot of a Mom's time goes into those outfits
So little Jack and Jane can collect candy bits
Although it's a colorful way to windup October
It's a reason for parents to remain quite sober!

Thankful in November

Thankful is what this November is all about
December costs so much you want to shout
Summer can be hot and dry out the brush
October can bring forest fires that seem to rush

November is cooler nights … a good night's sleep
Leaves fall from the Sycamores as if they weep
Orange, purple and browns collectively combine
God's handiwork is perfect, like eight before nine!

People seem happier when they are thankful
Gas prices are lower … so we buy a tank full
The Spirit of Holidays infiltrates our towns
Families invite friends as love surrounds!

It's a time to be thankful … for we have so much
Yet, let us not forget the less fortunate and such
And because we know not how our future ends
Be Thankful in November … for family and friends!

December:
Short Days and Bright Nights

December is all about seasonal fun
Albeit, it means the year is done
Faces are filled with wider smiles
Holiday lights are seen for miles

Seasonal hymns flow from the radio
Even strangers seem to say hello
Shops and malls market their gifts
Parking lots shuffle vehicles in shifts

Mothers and daughters walk in stride
Merchandise is stacked high and wide
"Sales" compete for every last dollar
Santa notices how the kids get taller

College football takes center stage
As students seek a part time wage
Internet Shoppers don't have to go
But, then again, there isn't any snow!

Many people go to parties and forego dinner
It's not easy to end the month a little thinner
What, with all the food and drink consumed
It's no wonder most December diets are doomed!

December 21st is the years' shortest day
Bright Christmas lights illuminate our way!
Christmas music reminds us of the reason
Christians treat the month like a religious season!

Love of Country

July 4th
Independence Day

A letter to the King simply said
The Colonies desired sovereignty instead
A brave declaration was signed that day
July 4th in the US of A

A national day of remembrance
To celebrate our independence
Could just as well be Patriots Day
July 4th in the US of A

In the year 1776 there was no parade
We were the one who needed Foreign aide
And even the French saw it our way
July 4th in the US of A

Good King George demanded more money
Paul Revere didn't think that was funny
And English tea was dumped in a bay
July 4th in the US of A

Now, it's fireworks, picnics and a parade
And we are the country who donates aide
For Liberty and Freedom this is the way!
July 4th in the US of A

My Flag …

My Flag is fifty stars and thirteen stripes
The logo of Freedom for those with gripes
Six stripes of white and seven of red
A nation conceived in liberty Lincoln said

My Flag is a beacon of hope to every refugee
Especially the oppressed seeking to be free
And for me … lucky enough to be born here
In mind and heart My Flag is incredibly dear

My Flag is a symbol of bravery and pride
So when called by my country I did not hide
Asked to defend it against a foreign power
I became an Armor Officer at the given hour

My Flag was raised on European Beaches
And battlefields as far as freedom reaches
As an Eagle Scout I learned to fold My Flag
To carry it high and not allow it to drag

My Flag has added stars as the years have past
But the number of stripes will always last
Allegiance to My Flag before God is my right
And I feel better when My Flag is in sight

A Salute to …
George Washington

George Washington was not only tall
He was obviously a leader above all
Dressed in his wig of white hair
He carried himself with quite a flair

He was President number one, of course
As General, he rode a huge white horse
And just when the British had it won
He came through like the favorite son

On the Delaware River he stood in the boat
Only because on ice … it need not float
But history recorded his fine leadership skills
And now he appears on our one dollar bills.

Mount Rushmore

Six Grandfathers mountain was originally its name
And renamed in 1885 for a New York lawyer of fame
Tons of its granite face by dynamite was blown
That the Congress funded it in 1927 is little known

Calvin Coolidge was president back then
And it was finished in '41 after four years and ten
Fortunately, not one of the 400 workers died
And now two million view it with national pride

A Danish-American, Gutzon Borglum, was asked
And he and a son, Lincoln, accepted the giant task
The 60 foot sculptures are 5,725 feet above the sea
But the 1,278 acre park is a wonderful place to be

Drive into the famous Black Hills, through a gate
On Highway 244 near Keystone, South Dakota state
And park near the visitor center in a very large lot
The entire memorial is located in a beautiful spot

Four presidents are enshrined in granite stone
Four of the very best our country has known
Washington and Jefferson are there to view
And Teddy and Abe are up there too

Veterans Day

There is nothing more "American"
Than being a Military Veteran
To wear our uniform with pride
To march in synchronized stride

Since early settlers came ashore
It's sad to say, there's always been war
For the past two-hundred fifty years
Veterans have had to face these fears

Yet, while others hid, and dared not go
For fear their fate they would not know
Our Veterans honorably answered the call
And now a day is set … to honor them all!

To make it possible our people to live
We've sent our best … their lives to give
It's the ultimate patriotic act
To be placed in harms way, in fact!

Since only the brave seem to qualify'
Even knowing some might die!
Isn't it about time we gave them a day
They deserve our "Thanks"; it's safe to say!

Memorial Day

Every year on the last Monday in May
Our war dead are honored on Memorial Day
An unknown soldier's grave is given a wreath
A moment of silence is given regardless of belief

So, what's so special about Memorial Day?
Do most Americans even honor it, anyway?
Is it just an excuse for the Post Office to close?
Could it be that it is more than all of those?

Ever since Plymouth Rock and Jamestown
Wars have called our young to be duty bound
Duty to themselves and duty to the US of A
To take up arms in support of the American way

While many have avoided the chance to serve
The few who did, this day of honor they deserve
For so many that gave the ultimate sacrifice
This national day of remembrance will have to suffice

On Memorial Day we take a moment to remember
Like those who paid the price in 1941, December
From Bunker Hill, Gettysburg, Iwo Jima and Baghdad
Our brightest and best deserve a day they never had

They deserve to be remembered on a very special day
And be saluted and honored in a very special way
On a national Memorial Day remembering life's strife
By all who have benefited … from every single life

Santa Barbara
Summer Scene

It was a warm June summer night
Pigeons and Gulls were seen in flight
The Coastal Range background was a hazy gray
Santa Barbara harbor rested in a beautiful bay

Expensive yachts were tied down tight
And the harbor below was bathed in soft light
Sloops and powerboats bobbed side by side
Some very narrow … and some very wide

In a sea of masts … each one very straight
The boats slept silently in patient wait
Lanyards and lines arranged in proper order
Each one its own purpose within its boarder

As if waiting for their skippers to each appear
Ships were in alignment parallel to the pier
Each one shone a female name on its stern
For such expensive toys … there is a lot to earn

Like others around me I slowly sipped my drink
It was a wonderful moment to just sit and think
The second floor bistro offered the perfect view
It was one of those times … too good to be true!

The Resort at Coeur d'Alene

One day in May when in the sun you'd bake
I drove to the resort on Coeur d'Alene lake
And there, too good to be true …
Is the resort with the most incredible view

So, into the Coeur d' Alene Resort I strode
Up to the 7th floor in an elevator I rode
To Beverly's Restaurant & Lounge I was drawn
Compelled like a salmon returning to spawn

Oh, my! What a beautiful breathtaking sight
The lake water glistened in early evening light
Through tall clear windows tinted and clean
A half-dozen run-abouts were a playful scene

Fifty foot firs lined the lake's boulder banks
For such natural beauty I give God the thanks
A dozen Canadian geese even flew by in a "V"
As the lake became grey as far as I could see

The warm May sun receded and boats were few
Daylight lingered long after dinner was through
But I'll never forget the kids jumping from rocks
And tourists strolling on the long wooden docks

The Plaza
At Arcata

A Plaza is a plot of ground
Historically renown
And most likely situated
in a small college town
In some cases there is not even
a tower for a clock
The Plaza in Arcata, California
takes up a whole city block

It's symmetrically designed
like a big square wheel
Cement paths make it look like
a public stamp or seal
At its hub is a twenty foot statue
of a famous pioneer
In this case, President McKinley,
thought to be dear

Old worn out oak and steel benches
are placed all about
To facilitate patrons reading
and talking throughout
Musical entertainers sit cross-legged
on a green grassy patch
As jugglers are seen practicing
their throw and catch

The plaza attracts very colorful people
to its' pretty city park
And the day crowd usually disappears
before it turns dark
Sadly, some men appear to be dirty
and not very clean
As scantily clad and barefooted women
can also be seen

Yet, it's amazing to me in this
21st century of time
That so many men and women
appear to not have a dime
You would hope that life need not
extract such a painful toll
In a quaint little American town
with my national flag on a pole

Sausalito View …
"Saved to Memory"

Once, after a job, I had some time before my flight
So, as I approached Sausalito I took the exit to the right
Only a few miles ahead stood the Golden Gate
Occasionally it feels good… to refresh my mind's state

I stopped at a harbor side café in Sausalito at noon
A winter sun reflected on the water … just like the moon
The "Rock", Bay Bridge and City sat on muted haze
As a world famous Bay glistened like diamonds ablaze

Gulls perched on pillars performed a vaudeville show
A soft cloudless sky silhouetted the city, San Francisco
I'm glad to have postponed my rush to leave
This moment of peace was nice to conceive

Although a parking meter was hard to find
Shops and galleries were extraordinarily kind
Visitors paused to photograph this digital delight
And I saved Sausalito "to memory" … before my flight

Special Memories

Lucky's Park

In a sweaty September summer sun
Lucky, a 110 pound "Newfy", can have fun
Perched on a throne of painted steel
His large black silhouette appears very real

Only a half dozen of the metal tables stand
But it's not about the tables on this sacred land
It's about the unique natural tranquility there
A place for people, animals and nature to share

As Lucky lay on the table with crossed paws
A sign at the parking lot sets forth the laws
Other breeds of dogs have walked by and looked
Very aware that this table was already booked

Huge sycamores and oaks stand guard
To find such a place you'd have to look hard
Their green canopy dilutes the sun's light
With the help of an elm it is soft … not bright

It is a special place not far from the shore
Where one can sit under a giant Sycamore
So sacred it's like a natural living shrine
So heavily shaded a sun can hardly shine

In a box canyon about four miles from the sea
A gentle cool breeze creates a nice place to be
Oaks and elms add to a canopy of green
A quarter mile of cement walkway is barely seen

A dry creek bed erodes the earth east to west
Its' community use is simply the very best
Soft afternoon light illuminates particles of dust
Allowing visitors to witness nature's lust

Beautifully designed with natural growth in mind
This six acre plot is one of the very best kind
A few steel tables are scattered about
As two dozen patrons are seen throughout

A large sign greets visitors at the parking lot
It sets out rules and regulations to do and do not
There is a bag dispenser to make it handy
Into which to deposit; all of one's dog-candy!

There's even a fenced area for children to play
Making it the perfect place for parents to stay
Only occasionally is the silence broken by a bark
What a perfect place for a neighborhood Dog Park

A Beach Afternoon

Afternoon fun
Under a San Diego Sun
Warm and clear
A cloud dared not appear

At La Jolla Shores beach
So convenient to reach
We found a spot for the car
On a street not far

In portable chairs
We watched other pairs
And read our books
As I enjoyed her looks

The ocean water was inviting
And there was a Kayak sighting
As along the tide line we walked
We held hands and talked

Early Dawn

The morning sunrise is a beautiful sight
Overhead is a pair of ducks in flight
On the golf course pond fifty feet below
Nature in putting on a jolly good show

Rays of sun light illuminate the west hill
The misty air above the valley is hazy still
I can hear a bravado base-echo of a Bull Frog
As synchronized Mallards dive toward his bog

The manicured golf course appears to be awake
As greens keepers freshen sand traps with a rake
A mist escapes the vanishing pool bedside me
The Maderas Golf Club is spectacular to see

Many species of birds increase their chirping
As the proud Bull Frog finally quits burping
A Blue Heron glides gracefully over the pond
The sun rises higher with a flick of God's wand

The valley below fills with the morning sun
The grounds keepers still have work to be done
Next to the pond a golf hole is moved on the green
Incredibly, God's Early Dawn is a gorgeous scene.

The Old Bernardo Winery

An amazing old winery is still alive and well in RB
On Sunday afternoon it has become *thee* place to be
Although, today, I experienced a dark-gray overcast sky
I was able to sit outside and watch neighbors come by

A classical jazz guitar warmed a cold winter air
The soloist was a virtuoso; I could only stare!
It was such a soothing and relaxing sound
I never felt the need to get up and walk around

Tucked in amongst two dozen wooden boutiques
You feel the same warm friendliness of antiques
Under an old barn-wood roof many people can sit
While on nearby trees and shrubs white lights are lit!

Plenty of patio heaters removed the damp winter chill
A warm, cozy, ambiance spawned an entertainment thrill
The adults were as diverse and polite as I had seen
The cabernet sauvignon I sipped … was superbly keen!

Sunday afternoons at **Old Bernardo Winery** are fun
Most weekends you'll find … a lot of San Diego sun
It's a joy to chat and relax with red or white wine!
To make it even better, the price is affordably fine!

I like it because of the variety of people I can meet
Although, I noticed that wine drinkers don't *Tweet*
In fact, there was not a cell phone within my sight
No wonder this enchanted place … is a heavenly delight!

Dove Hunting

They arrive on August 31st of every year
An annual migration of shotguns and beer
Thousands of Hunters descend on a town
Most are dressed in camouflage and brown

They flood the restaurants needing to eat
And park their campers on every street
High on tradition they share stories of old
Embellishing tales each time they're told

It's still dark when these immigrants rise
That they've had little sleep is no surprise
To the shooting fields they need to be first
A half hour before sun rise shells will burst

The shooters set up in fields out of town
Intent on keeping the birds off the ground
Hopefully their stations are far enough apart
To prevent being shot, in the days' early start

At dawn, the small swift birds begin to fly
Most hunters need dozens to come by
To be able to put a limit of ten in their bag
The quantity of doves must definitely not lag

As intense desert temperatures quickly rise
Hunters walk slowly to pick up their prize
In a matter of minutes it can all be done
And if a limit is bagged, the hunter has won!

Each One a Champion

At last, it's here, the U.S. Open Tennis Championships
But without the strawberries 'n' cream or fish 'n' chips
No VIP boxes … sell out crowds … or expensive seats
It's just a chance to see the world's best tennis athletes!

Held in San Diego, California in Two Thousand and Two
At a fabulous tennis center bathed by a sky of baby blue
From around the world, players travel many miles
And they all bring along their natural, incredible smiles!

Truly an amazing and extraordinary sporting event!
It's a class act even without a sponsor's hospitality tent
Both men and women, young and old …come to play
After each round, only the winning sides get to stay!

There is no TV contract; the winners' checks are small
In this great tournament that's just not important at all.
These athletes compete hard … tennis players they are.
Some even excel and become an international star.

During the week, good sportsmanship's not hard to find.
Regardless of the score, line calls are generously kind.
Each one a champion at heart, their very souls they bare!
Because each player is strapped into a sports-wheelchair!

One Way to Meet a Lady

Oops, did I just see what I think I just saw … here?
Are my eyes tricking my mind after only one beer?
Kind of an interesting place, however, to meet.
It's certainly not like we just met on the street.

I was confused when I opened the door and saw you.
Standing there in the door, I didn't know what to do.
And yet, you were composed and looked so calm.
At that instant, I was the one with the sweaty palm!

You just stood there, smiled and seemed so polite.
I tried to hold back the laughter with all my might.
Even though, at the time, I hardly knew what to say.
For me, this was certainly a very memorable day.

It was the Claim Jumper Restaurant, just the same.
This just might give all new meaning to the name.
But even with such an obvious sign on the door,
You surprised me, standing in the middle of the floor.

Once, in college, I made the same mistake myself.
It can happen to anybody regardless of wealth.
I don't want you to think this casts a shadow of gloom.
It's not often a pretty blonde is found in a Men's Room!

Author's Note: Yes, this is a true story!!

"Order Number 98 …
   Please!"

It is comforting to know
My food is soon to show
Even though the line is long
With my number … I can't go wrong

My number tells me where I stand
It allows me to pick a table and land
It even gives me time to select a drink
With my number … I don't have to think

Get a number and time goes fast
A string of numbers doesn't last
It seems even when I have to wait
With my number … I won't be late

An anonymous voice will ring out
A number he, or she, will shout
It always rings in a pleasant voice
With my number … I have no choice

"Order number 97… Please!"
Ah, my taste buds this will tease
At least I don't have long to wait
Because … my number is 98!

Author's Note: *Order Number 98, Please*

This was another fun piece to write. I found myself in an "In and Out Burger" shop because I like their product. I always order the *"No. 2,"* with grilled onions! It is a Cheeseburger, Fries, and Drink for less than $5.00. I like to get my root beer drink and a couple cups of Ketchup for my fries. I grab three napkins and find a table or stool. Then I pour a spot of drink on my eating area and wipe it clean with one of the napkins; I use the same system every time!

On this occasion I think I had my Writing Journal with me, so I started to look around and write. My poems are normally just a written opinion of what I feel and see. Thus,, the name "Reflections of Life."

I will let you in on another little secret; my number was not really "98." I just used that number because when I got to the end of the poem I needed something that rhymed with "wait!"

It took me about ten more trips to the same shop to finally get a number close to that, but when I heard "98" announced I asked the patron to give it to me! I photocopied it for my original page!

A Cabin on the Lake
And the Wisconsin State Bird

We drove back East when Warren was only four
Little did he know how much fun was in store
To the Gran family farm outside Worthington town
And Pioneer Village which was world re-known

There were Grandpa's two huge chicken houses to see
And corn and soy bean fields were visible as far as could be
Acres and acres of crops arose from ground moist and dark
Evidence that God's germination plan is definitely no lark

Grandpa showed us chickens no older than two weeks
And how he vaccinated them and trimmed their beaks
It took 13 weeks before the chicks were old enough to lay
Then he ordered another ten thousand … to come and stay!

Grandpa Grann gave us a tour of an old Pioneer Village
That cold winter blizzards must have attempted to pillage
He was the proud appointed Mayor of that historical spot
And enjoyed guiding tourists in the town's preserved lot

Next we went on to see his cousins of nearly the same age
Greg and Bruce were about five and three at this stage
They lived in a nice two story at 2700 Lamplighter Lane
With a dog who thought he should've been a Great Dane!

Greg was the alpha dude and always wanted to trade
For a cowboy vest of Warren's a trade was made!
We arrived in Wisconsin on a lake guarded by birds
"Those are mosquitoes," were Dr. Brad's exact words!

"Now you've seen the Wisconsin state bird, boys"
We stayed inside and played with indoor games and toys!
The "State Birds" were about and the sun was very spotty
I can still remember Bruce … sitting in the outdoor potty

Mom took pictures of Dad teaching Warren to shoot a bow
The boys laughed and played … and soon … it was time to go!
Greg was older and he gave the ball a very good ride
Bruce was also very athletic, a fact he couldn't hide!

Days later the Johnson's drove us to their cabin on a lake
Grandma Grann brought along some home made cake
It was Warren's first attempt at baseball to play
But in a fenceless back yard the ball wouldn't stay

At Summer Camp

Not Deprived
I arrived
By Bus
Without fuss

To Stay
To Play
To Learn
To Discern

A Treat
To Meet
Other Boys
New Toys

In Sun
To Run
Physically Employed
I Enjoyed

The Little Angels
Of
Sandy Hook

Oh, Jesus, Son of Man
At your side I need to stand
Something terrible just went wrong
Twenty Little Angles have lost their song

In a tiny New England country town
Sandy Hook school turned upside down
Where little children used to stand
Now they wait to trust in your hand

The result of an unbelievable day
School children were said to pray
Now parents and families sadly mourn
Their hearts and minds surely torn

In neighborhood churches candles are lit
All over our country people see fit
Flowers and memorials are on display
Please, Jesus, expedite these angels without delay

Too young to have charted their course
I rely on you for their eternal life source
Lord, be on the watch for twenty tiny sails
And may the parents be assured … your love never fails

Easter Remembered
… As a Boy

As I recall the Easter Sundays of my youth
I was thankful to live in SoCal … not Duluth

It was traditional Presbyterian fare
And colorful spring hats were there

We drove across town to grandfather's house
Me, my brother, my father and Mom, his spouse

In those days, women's nylons had a seam
And Gaga's nursery rhymes allowed us to dream

Outside, we were drawn to the patio fish pond
Where bright orange fish encouraged us to bond

Grandpa and Dad lit smelly cigars after a meal
I was excited to able to wear the round paper seal

There were bulky box cameras made by Brownie
In the late 1940's we didn't have things by Sony

Finally, a colored egg hunt was spread o'r the lawn
Yes, Easter was a nice day for God's love to spawn

Grandpa's Favorites

The "Homeless"

We call them the "Homeless"
Not to be confused with "Hopeless"
Because they appear to wander about
"Please Help," you'd expect them to shout!

On city streets … in doorways sleep
So many … they seem like sheep
With sad countenance and outstretched hand
One wonders how long … they've had to stand

Daily they suffer their community's wrath
Most haven't, in weeks, had a bath
Torn, second-hand clothes are stained with dirt
Months pass without a clean sock or shirt!

Some pile objects high on a bike
Some use a back pack, as if on a hike
Many accumulate only what they carry
Others use a grocery cart … their goods to ferry

Their suffering sub-culture is much too large
Silently … society itself picks up the "charge"
A census for the homeless is quite unknown
Interest from Congress has never been shown

Wishing them invisible, whenever we drive by
We accept their presence, like clouds in the sky
And although they seem to have nothing to do
Our "Homeless" neighbors are God's children too!

Author's Note: *The "Homeless"*

This subject touches my heart! I tried to leave you with a little bit of hope for the unfortunate. The New Testament mentions several situations like those described in the poem! Tragically, history has recorded the fact that every society, that has had some sort of organized government, has experienced a portion of its population becoming homeless, for one reason or another. Whether caused by economic downturn and job loss, personal health, negligence, or just plain bad luck, some people stumble and fall through the cracks of comfort and well-being to a life of hardship.

Just the other day, I was approached in the parking lot of my local market by a man about thirty-five years of age. He was carrying an eight month old girl that was clean and very adorable. He had tattoos all over his neck and arms, and was standing next to a young woman of less than thirty years, but of average appearance. He introduced her as his wife and the mother of the baby and two other children not present. He rattled off a sad story of starting a new job as a welder, but having his first paycheck held back by his employer for another week. He asked for money to get he and his family to his first check. Normally, I would turn away, but this time I made the decision to take them into the grocery store and buy a gift certificate; it would allow the man and his "wife" to choose some baby supplies and the food of their choice. They thanked me, and then I turned and walked out!

Author's Note:

These next seven poems were written to record, in chronological order, those precious moments when I learned I was going to become, or had become, a Grandpa. These are some of the most monumental moments of my life, and they each brought me a feeling of pride, jubilation, joy, and happiness.

The Call!

At 10:15 am, May 7th, I got the call
The very good news … as told to all
Warren's Karen is now with child
And my reaction … anything but mild!

Into my phone I could only scream
Such happiness I could only dream
My face was flooded with one big tear
Thank you, Lord, for such a great year!

I can't wait to be a Grandpa-Pappy
My life recently has become so happy
As the cycle of life continues to turn
The baby's sex we will very soon learn!

Grandpa Glenn

A Grandpa's Prayer!
... Leela Arrives

Lord ... about my grandchild!
The day's finally *here!*
Cute little Leela arrived in style ...
I'm a Grandfather ... *oh, dear!*

Seems only yesterday
that word got *out* ...
to expect a child
who's sex was in *doubt!*

For nine long months
the child has *grown!*
Thanks to you, Lord ...
the sex is now *known!*

And since I'd like more ...
than just one of *these,*
I prayerfully petition you
to encourage this again, please!

Amen, Grandpa Glenn

One More Christmas Gift!

At 7:10 pm, December 25th, I was told
By my Grand Daughter Leela … a four year old
As instructed by Warren, her dad
That there was one more gift I had!

I was already feeling good this Christmas night
Yet the best was yet to come … to my delight
I had eaten a big dinner and a piece of pie
To the Choate family we had just said "Good Bye"

Earlier, Santa had been seen with gifts at the door
I was very slow … just getting off the floor!
Sure enough, there was Santa … waving a hand
But being in a hurry … off he ran

Later, I left with Warren's family to see their new car
It was parked down the block … but not too far
As Warren buckled Leela into her safety seat
He told her to tell me … of one more treat

As I leaned in to listen to Leela's gentle voice
She whispered in my ear as if by choice
"Yes," she said quite certain, "it wasn't a maybe"
"Next June, we're going to have a baby"!

PS: "Thank you, God, for this very special child …
        Next June my heart will obviously run wild
        Your miracle of life is a wonder to behold
        It was very nice that from Leela I was told!"

Amen, Grandpa Glenn

A Phone Call About Sex!

At 4:00 p.m., June 10th, Two Thousand Ten
I answered my phone, "Hi, this is Glenn!"
Then I realized it was Warren, my son
Excitedly, I listened … to what had been done!

It seems a Doctor had let the "cat out of the bag"
And now Warren was playing telephone info tag
Evidently, Karen's Doctor had let it be known
What Karen at her appointment … had been shown

My Grandbaby's sex was known only to him
However, his ability to keep a secret was a bit too slim
Forgetting the parent's desire … not to know …
He mentioned an appendage that seemed to show!

So, Karen came home, her countenance all aglow
Confident her family would also want to know!
As she explained to Leela in a very loving way
Warren's dream came true … of having a son one day!

A Grandpa's Prayer II!
"Late can mean more!"

Dear, Lord … just so you know …

A little late, and surrounded in love, the baby arrived
For over nine months it had miraculously survived!
In a natural, perfect environment; warm and wet
Warren's wife, Karen, was ready … everything was set.
Rumor had it, big sister Leela had even called out …
"Come out, come out." she did shout.
"I want to talk to you!"
Like her beautiful mother, Leela was anxious too!

Meanwhile, Warren worked wonders on their house
With some encouragement from his pregnant spouse!
He completely re-modeled the second floor … upstairs
A two-bed room now matches Leela and her bears!
These past few months, Karen's health was very good
Eating and exercising like she knew she should …
Doctors monitored the baby to determine its' date
Who'd have guessed the delivery … to be so late!

But "late" obviously can mean "grows more"
Oh, my, what surprises You had in store!
On its due date, eleven days prior, the weight was eight
Who knew to add two ounces a day if it was late!
By mistake … a doctor let "the Cat out of the Bag!"
Evidently, one anatomical part had a distinctive tag
So before the birth, this time, the baby's sex was known
It seems that Warren's male gene … had finally shown!

Amen, Grandpa Glenn

A Phone Call from an Angel!

October 3rd, 2012; I was watching a presidential Debate
At 6:40 PM television history would have to wait
My Blackberry cell said it was Warren, my son
At least it wasn't some contest I supposedly had won!

"Hi, Grandpa Glenn, it's Leela" her angelic voice said
"Oh, it's you, Leela; isn't it about time you were in bed?"
"Did you have a nice time at your school today?"
"Does your little brother, River, still get in your way?"

"Isn't it a little bit late to be calling on the phone?"
"I hope you are not at home by yourself, all alone!"
"No, Grandpa that is not why I called!"
I stood next to my bed aghast and appalled

"So what do I owe the pleasure of your call?"
I loved hearing her voice… I tried to stall
"Mommy and Daddy said I could to tell"
"That Mommy in fine and all is well"

"We're going to have another baby next year"
Her vocabulary was mature, yet sweet and dear
"Oh, Leela, that is wonderful news," I said
I realized then … I was the one who needed a bed!

 PS: "Thank you, God, for another new child …
           Next April my heart will again run wild
           Your creation of life is a miracle above all
           What a nice surprise to receive Leela's call !"
Amen, Grandpa Glenn

One Push! Aka, "O.P."

Your first breath of air
Was on a day warm and fair
Although a few days late
It was an exciting wait!

Your Daddy saw you first … I think
Only **One Push** and faster than a wink
You left a dark warm tummy
Still attached to your lovely mommy

The 19th of April was a very good day
To take center stage in life's grand play
With all your essential *parts* in tact
You were very beautiful, that's a fact!

If down the road, you ever start to yelp
Leela and Deacon-River will be there to help
You were born in the Spring instead of Fall
And all too soon, you'll be gorgeous and tall

Wonderful parents will bath you in love
Meanwhile, you'll also be loved … by God above
Since I know not what your name will be
I will simply call you … my little "O.P."!

PS: "Thank you, Karen and Warren …
       For creating such a beautiful and
       loving home to raise three gorgeous
       human beings! You truly are …
       amazing parents!

Love, Grandpa Glenn

Pajama Baby

She is affectionately called "Pajama Baby"!
A symbol of love and affection, maybe!

Pajama Baby is a simple, brown cloth doll
To be hugged … not thrown like a ball!

Her cover is grey, canvas-like cloth.
She does not have claws... like a sloth!

With a smooth, tan, plastic head,
She is Leela's favorite to take to bed!

Only about ten inches in height,
She has painted blue eyes for sight!

Like most dolls, she can play in a swing.
Wouldn't it be nice if she could also sing!

Precious to hold, she is soft and cuddly
Her plain little body is very snuggly!

The name, Pajama Baby, has a happy sound
And her love for Leela abounds all around

Although she sometimes ends up on the floor
She's in Leela's arms if a knock at the door!

A Mother and Daughter

Wow, what a fabulous time!
And to think, it didn't cost a dime!
To drop by Little Leela's house
And visit my son's Lovely Spouse!

Mother and Daughter a love share
Something Leela is very much aware!
The relationship is so totally sweet
Such a scene is a glorious treat!

The ultimate in Love and Trust
Security is still her mother's bust!
As the world on its axis turns
It's amazing how fast Leela learns

Her small hand reaches for another
In order to cross a street together
She knows Mom's hand is always there
As well as her loving ... heart to share!

Fatherhood is …

Being a very proud DAD
Glad for the small child … I once had
Feeding a cute face with a tiny spoon
Knowing growth would come … way to soon!
Fatherhood is …
Setting up a slot car track down a hall
Taking time to show … how to hit a ball
Grateful to God to be able to teach
And watch him dig at a sandy beach
Fatherhood is …
Watching him sit on his Grandpa's knee
And noticing how attentive … he could be
Reading aloud his favorite books
Explaining how heroes capture crooks
Fatherhood is …
Building a playhouse in which to play
Totally amazed at words he would say
Coaching a team on which he starred
Receiving a precious Dad's Day card
Fatherhood is …
Insisting he taste his fresh green peas
Teaching him to sing his A,B,C's
Seeing him pulled by a toy poodle, his pet.
Remembering the first moment we met!
Fatherhood is …
Feeling excited for a son hunting his first dove
Noticing his eyes express his love
Playing Marco Polo with an underwater fish
Hoping come true … his every wish!

Through Dad's Eyes

It's great being Warren's DAD
The best experience I've ever had
T'was an honor right from the start
Of course, God played a really big part

So many times I've given thanks to God
Watching Warren play on a field of sod
So cute in shorts and long blue socks
I felt sorry when he got the Chicken pocks

Actually, it's his Mother I need to thank
But it was my idea to build him a tank
Big enough to hide-in with a tire on top
He'd play all day and would rarely stop

From day one he was a happy little guy
He'd meet kids easily and wasn't very shy
Even though I think he was born to be a leader
I remember the day we built a bird feeder

Wearing my army jacket was really fun
We lived in Tacoma and rarely was there sun
But when he put on my helmet; what a sight
He was like a Green Beret training at night

Just to hear him call me DAD
Makes getting older not so bad
And now that he has a family and a house
I'm thrilled that Karen is his spouse

Before I Say "Good Bye"

Thanks, God, for taking my call
Life is great, I'm having a ball
Things seem to be going my way
Yet, there's so much I want to say.

A good friend of mine died today
And I just saw him yesterday
We said, "Hello" in Starbucks RB
I pray OK his wife and sons will be

He was really a very nice guy
He always smiled when I said "Hi"
Oh, Dear God, what can I do?
Before my life is finally through

I feel the need to remind my son
Before my life is finally done
How proud I am to be his DAD
What a wonderful life I've really had!

LOVE, DAD

Dedicated to my fellow Realtor,
husband and father, who died
of a heart attack earlier today!
He was in the prime of his career!
Nov. 10, 2005

A Valentine's Day Hug …
For Grandpa

If the AARP was to be polled
You'd find what you've been told
That although they can't eat the candy
A Valentine's Day hug is really Dandy

Oh, sure, the usual stuff is fine
Old folks like roses and wine
Even a thoughtful card is still OK
They're used to Valentine's Day!

But if you appreciate your baby sitter
That old electrician or the pipe fitter
Add pleasure to that card or letter
By giving a hug that's even better!

Hugs are a wonderful expression of joy
They last longer than a Valentine Toy
Hugging Grandpa is like giving part of you
And who knows, you might even get one too

A Grandpa's Day at the Zoo

It helps to have a three year old Grand Daughter, Leela
And a beautiful, tall, intelligent Daughter-in-Law too!
To act as your tour guides around all the grounds
Of the fabulous, world famous, San Diego zoo!
First, we took a high wire ride across the sky
In a very durable gondola that seated four!
It allowed a wonderful panoramic view
Although, there's even so much more!
The elephants on exhibit are huge
Though they're not tallest of all
That prize goes to the giraffes
But they can't stand on a ball!
The polar bears are giants too
Growing to over eight feet tall
And they can play in the water
With a large, purple, rubber ball!

And yet, one of the best zoo thrills
Is watching how apes use their toes!
A large silver-back male is dominant
With a gigantic head and big flat nose!
His family of apes is hilarious to watch
Some sleep while others play in the grass.
One large female likes to eat bamboo shoots
While resting herself against the Grotto glass!
There are also many types of antelope and deer
There are lions and tigers and all types of cats
There're snakes, lizards and things that crawl
There are Pandas, Birds and nocturnal Bats
To see all the animals in one visit is hard
It isn't necessary in one day to see it all
Because it is so much fun to visit there
I want go again … and have a ball!

An Alpha Phi in Aisle Eight!

T'was Vons Market; the day wasn't late
We met by chance … in aisle number eight
I was price shopping juice … nothing more
I asked, "What's best, three for five or two for four?"

She had a collegiate look … cute and blond
On her lips a friendly smile she donned
We exchanged mundane remarks at first
I thought not about my juice or thirst

The conversation turned to something canned
A small round can without a metal band
Luckily for me I had seen it only moments ago
I led and she followed; albeit fast not slow

We discussed her need for Tuna then
I didn't mention I liked it on rice … by Uncle Ben
She thanked me and we talked some more
I kept asking, "Three for five or two for four?"

She'd already told me "three for five" was best
Little did she know … it had been a test!
Before we left the tuna I knew she'd taught school
Which only confirmed … she wasn't a fool

We walked to her car and I took a picture
I bragged I was published but didn't lecture
We talked about college days and continued to chatter
The fact she was an Alpha Phi … was even better!

More Starbucks

The Old General Store

White puffy clouds scarcely dot a light blue sky
On the patio at Starbucks my neighbors walk by
The morning air is still; the temperature is warm
Fallen pastry crumbs allow blackbirds to swarm

Sunday morning people show up to sit and talk
Albeit, it's an excuse for some joggers to walk
Even the choir, between services, can be seen
There are some students, and an occasional dean

Real Estate agents check their newspaper's ad
The market is rising sharply, buyers are sad!
Mortgage brokers sit with a big smile on their face
Interest rates are so low, they love this place!

Stock brokers are bewildered as assets depreciate
Some of their clients want to blame the State
Ex-military men discuss the possibility of war
Young girls with ankle tattoos think it's a bore!

This is what our ancestors liked to do, too
No TV, radio, or rap; the idea is really not new
Solving world problems with friends, you see …
Is like *The Old General Store* … advice is free!!

PS: This was written on a Sunday morning
at the Rancho Bernardo Starbucks (across the
parking lot from Vons Market) in 2003
before the invasion of Iraq.

The Starlings of Starbucks

At *Starbucks*, even the black Starlings like to table hop!
If there is pastry to snatch the birds will fly by and stop.
They check out the coffee customers who are meeting.
But their primary purpose would be that of a greeting!

The flying daredevils swoosh above the patio with ease.
Darting around patrons whose crumbs seem to tease.
But turn a head and from nowhere a flock will appear.
They're all quite daring, and they perch incredibly near!

Though customers come and go, the tiny birds do thrive.
Amazing, intelligent acrobats, they know when to arrive.
These fine, feathered flighty creatures just seem to know.
At the possibility of a morsel they swoop down and go!

Brave and stealth to be sure, they know when to hide.
They use the rules of engagement by which they abide.
They groom the ground and tables throughout the day.
And with tilted heads appear to say, "Is everything OK?"

Thanksgiving
at Starbucks

Yes, Martha, there is Thanksgiving at Starbucks too
Since the need for fellowship is not entirely new
Although the coffee and cakes will not be free
The shop will be open from seven to three!

My friends and I will rely on others to bake
The nice selection of doughnuts and coffee cake
Each morning pastry items are all lined up in trays
Other food items are displayed several different ways

They have a new location in Rancho Bernardo
Across from the gas station that makes my car go
The staff is very nice and they treat you like a king
They offer with each hot drink a paper cup ring

Thanksgiving day the store is rather quiet
As long as the coffee is hot people buy it
Along with holiday lattes of pumpkin and spice
The soft, smooth jazz is comfortable and nice

Sandwiches of high fiber bread are nice 'n' tasty
But with my coffee I normally have a pastry
It's a fine, friendly place to meet while I drink
Or just work on my poetry, as I sit and think!

Starbucks …
In Summer

t's summer … the patio is very hot
The air is dry … rained it has not
Inside the store, Starbucks is cool
Sight of Frappuccinos cause drool

Most chairs are occupied
At Starbucks nothing is fried
Good food is always on hand
Temptation lingers in a glass stand

Merchandise is packed high
Positioned for someone to buy
Music sounds are soothing and soft
Inviting … like a San Francisco loft

While some people sit and read
Others just sip and their faces feed
Small groups nod and chatter
A mom smiles at her kid's laughter

Starbucks creates a friendly place
It draws people with a happy face
Coffee and chocolate can easily mix
Especially for those who crave … a caffeinated fix.

Starbucks Ice
and Summer Heat

T'was over 100 degrees of heat today
Hot enough to suck one's breathe away
With dense clouds that were suppressive
The hot sun was most impressive

People walk much more slowly
Folks at bus stops look tired and lonely
Birds don't even seem to want to fly
Kids in school probably ask why

Meanwhile …
Starbucks foot traffic is a steady flow
Today, three ice smoothies I got to know
My favorite drink is still Strawberries and Cream
For anything better I can only dream!

Good Mooorrrning … Starbucks!

"Have a nice day!" … Hello!
"Good morning … Hi!
Outside a Starbucks shop door
My neighbors walk by

Every few seconds …
It's a constant parade
All shapes and sizes
Seeking a caffeine aide!

Morning sun … a cloudless sky
Mid-September … seven to nine
An affluent congregation
Inside, a never ending line!

Suites and ties arrive
Shorts, tees and sandals too
Some work … and some do not
Occasionally, a mom with a tot

A heavy glass door
A sign that says "Pull"
Smooth jazz floats in the air
The parking lot is full!

"Hi" …"Good Morning!"
"Have a nice day!
It brings a smile to my lips
To greet people this way!

Mother's Day at Starbucks

On Mother's Day moms are singled out
Children are to be obedient and not to pout
Dads show appreciation with breakfast in bed
As kids cuddle their moms, nice things are said

Many moms relax at Starbucks coffee house
Lots of kids are treating Dad's happy spouse
Since they're honored this special Sunday
Today … moms should not have to pay!

Women approach a counter for coffee and a bun
As tiny toddlers tug, their moms are having fun
Twitching in line, touching everything twice
Obviously, God made moms patient and nice

Preschoolers seem aware and hold mom's hand
As teenagers sacrifice the need for an I-Pod band
It's great to see families give moms a brake
After all, God created moms for all our sake

It's Saturday Morning

It's Saturday morning, I'm in a Starbucks shop
It's a place for my neighbors and I to table hop
A friendly atmosphere draws the people out
Some even discuss what the world's all about!

In post 9-11, Rancho Bernardo needs this place
It's all about coffee, and greetings, face to face
No TV or cartoons; just a clean, cool, casual air
Sitting here reminds me of being at a street fair!

Saturday, all makes and models of folks show up
Some bring a pet bird, and some a small pup
Mothers bring a daughter, fathers bring a son
All using Saturday morning to enjoy some fun!

I sit in the corner, sipping my mocha, with my pad
Jotting down things around me; I'm very glad
To watch all the different people pass through
Warms my heart and makes me proud of what I do!

Tee shirts and shorts is definitely the norm
Unlike, Seattle, you dress for the next storm
It's Saturday; people are happy enjoying their day
What a great place we live in, to sip coffee and play!

It's about my CuP

My new CuP is quite essential to me
It's more than just for others to see
It's my Teddy Bear
It's my soft blanket with the tiny tear

I love my CuP
It's akin to a faithful pup
I take it with me wherever I go
What it contains I always know

I really enjoy the new plastic style
With my CuP I always seem to smile
The lid's lip is curved; I love its' smooth feel
The design needs not … a rubber seal

When I walk into Starbucks and wave
I just grin and know I'm going to save
Why, they allow me to pay even less
With my CuP I'd gladly pay more I confess

They wash it out and get it ready
And give it back full with a hand that is steady
When I give them my Gold Card and smile
They know my CuP will return in a very short while!

Animals:
Real and Imaginary

Mr. Giraffe

When you think of Mr. Giraffe … you normally think tall
However, unlike a seal, on his nose he can't catch a ball
He uses tall, skinny legs to walk, run, or stand
Mr. Giraffe is the world's tallest animal to walk on land

Being tall is made up of several different things
Mr. Giraffe has a long neck and a nose without rings
Little horns even protrude from quite a large head
I hope he's able to sleep ... in a very long and grassy bed

Mr. Giraffe has to be cautious … since he's easily spotted
Lucky for him … his skin is camouflaged and dotted
His height is an advantage when standing among trees
He can reach leaves 'n' berries known to birds and bees!

Even though lions and leopards do not worry about tall
Except for a cheetah … giraffes can outrun them all
That's why they hang around with elephants so much
Giraffes feel safer … if they graze in a bunch!

Mr. Giraffe has very long and pointed "elf-like" ears
The fact he can hear so well must dispel most fears
And have you ever in your life seen a tongue so long
A tongue, a foot and a half long, must be strong!

Yet, nobody has ever complained about a Giraffe's bark
I think stories of a barking giraffe are a laughable lark
The fact is, Mr. Giraffe is as quiet as a tiny field mouse
Which is probably why he is so loved by his spouse!

The American Buffalo

An American Buffalo wears a thick brown winter coat
Like you would on a windy sea … in very small boat
It resembles a Male Lion's long hairy mane
Like if you spilled coffee … it probably wouldn't stain

When it snows on a Buffalo's hairy skin it doesn't melt
Which is one reason the American Indian hunted its' pelt
In fact, when the white man went west, the land to claim
Millions of the large animals lived in herds on the plain

By the year 1900, Buffalo in America were hard to find
But new government laws have been good and kind
By the year 2000 they numbered over 200,000 and ten
Without conservation where would they have been?

The Buffalo should really be called an American Bison
But not to be confused with frozen chickens by Tyson
However, some butcher shops still offer Buffalo meat
Some say it's delicious and like it for an occasional treat

American Bison or Buffalo, on grasses it likes to feast
It also weighs more than any other North American beast
Yet it took an act of Congress to secure the Buffalo's fame
On a Nickel is imprinted the Buffalo's picture and name

The Beautiful Birds

Birds are entirely different from any living thing
Sure, most of them fly… but they also sing!
Although some warble, some chirp, and some coo
It is truly a blessing to listen to what the Birds do!

A Humming bird will seem in flight to flutter
Much like a moth stuck in some butter!
A Hawk will spread huge wings and glide
Knowing its' pray can not possibly hide!

A Mourning Dove whistles when it takes to flight
Regardless if it is morning, noon or night!
The House Finch skips through the air
Where there is one, there is usually a pair!

Male Mallard Ducks are a beautiful sight
Their green florescence heads glisten in light!
Smaller Bufflehead Ducks are easy to spot
They have little white heads with a black eye dot!

An Owl's wings flap silently … slowly in the dark
Its howl is much different from a Meadow Lark!
A huge flock of Crows can darken the sky
All chatting loudly at dusk when they fly!

When you consider the Physics of it all
You can understand why … birds don't fall!
So the next time you look up into the sky
Just be grateful … that cows can't fly!

The Enormous Elephant

An Elephant is obviously a very big thing
So big in fact, it doesn't need to bite or sting
Its' enormous size helps to protect it
But in small places, its' trunk will fit!

Elephants are fun to watch at the zoo
Especially if … they're more than two
They seem to shuffle around kind of slow
It's like they don't have … a place to go!

When they are thirsty they sure can drink
They suck up water in their trunk, I think
It's no wonder they don't cough and sneeze
But when they drink, they don't say "Please"!

The Elephants at the zoo are always Gray
But I don't think it's … from eating hay
They seem to sway when slowly they walk
I wish the Elephants in the zoo … could talk!

The "Sweet" Bee

For nature's perfect insect I'd nominate the Honey Bee!
They're smarter and work harder than insects we see
They've a social structure from a Queen on down
Worker Bees live to maintain a hive and not a frown

And yet, Honey Bees frequently land on a tennis court
It must be the blue color that causes them to abort!
It's like they give up on their job they know they must do
If they ever met a lawyer, I wonder if they'd suit!

Ever wondered why they land in a swimming pool?
To get them out you need a special tool!
They know they can't swim, so why do they try?
Once out of the pool their wings have to dry!

They have an incredible sense of direction
I doubt if they ever make a GPS correction
They know exactly the location of their hive
 So why in a swimming pool do they need to dive?

Honey Bees are nice little fellows, that is for sure
The sweet smell of pollen must be an insatiable lure
They hover over flowers their honey to gather
 If I worked that hard I'd get soaked in a lather!

Of course, most people appreciate the job they do
If you don't like honey, I wouldn't want to be you
On hot buttered toast, fresh honey is a very nice treat
All things considered, Honey Bees can't be beat!

The Lion

Of all the giant cats, the Lion is King
Seen in a circus, they perform in a caged ring
Usually in a sports arena or under a giant tent
From an African country to America … they are sent

The Lion even has his own movie and song
With a name like "Lion King", who could go wrong?
Recall the story of Simba, the Lion cub prince
And his scary uncle Scar, who made Simba wince

 Every adult male grows a long hairy mane
The larger the mane, the less they suffer pain
A Lion's thick mane swells his body, as it should!
That is scares other Lions, is clearly understood

To a ferocious looking male it's all about his "Pride"
Hopefully, up to a dozen females will stay by his side
Meanwhile, young males watch, and see how it's done
To become the Alpha Lion, in a fight he must have won!!

It is the female Lion that hunts on the African plain
But they'll let the male eat first, if they're wise and sane
A male Lion's territory looks like a comfortable place
But the truth is, he's constantly on guard for his space!

The Polar Bear …
At home on ice

What is very big and white
Walks in the Northern Light
With paws incredibly big
And able in ice to dig?

You wonder why I even must ask
Only one is up to the task
When its' best meal is a baby seal
Living on ice is part of the deal

Hunting alone is part of a solitary life
The male bear prefers not to keep a wife
Even though its' color matches white snow
How it survives I'll never know

It looks powerful when it walks
But in books you'd think it talks
With eyes alert and a friendly grin
In a race with a man it will always win

In a zoo they're a favorite of so many
Their picture should probably be on our penny
A bronze sculpted image I dream to stare
Thankful Noah remembered the Polar Bear!

An Elephant and Giraffe … is an *Eleraffe*

Ever seen an **Eleraffe**?
With a neck like a Giraffe
It eats grasses and hay
Most often it's gray

Its' trunk can be a hose …
Or used to sniff like a nose!
It has big ears that flop …
Its' round feet go "Plop-plop"

It is such a tall beast
Its' not afraid …in the least!
It can reach the tallest trees
And run like the breeze

Undoubtedly big …
Much larger than a pig!
With a long spotted trunk …
It's a very large hunk!

But, I sometimes wonder …
If God was to blunder
and create such a thing …
Would it do tricks in a ring?

A Skunk
and a Rabbit…
Is a Skabbit!

It is most often seen around our home
Living underground in a hole like a dome
They come out at night after dark
They are silent and quiet, they never bark

Like a Skunk, they have a white stripe on their back
And a big bushy tail they do not lack
They love to eat grass and carrots, but eat no meat
For a Skabbit, a salad would be a very nice treat

At first, they look kind'a scary as they scurry
But they are gentle and have a coat that is fury
Except for its white stripe its color is rather tan
Which enables it to blend in with brown and tan sand

Because it is only out at night
During the day they hide out of sight
Skabbits are fast and have very long ears
They can hear very well and lack many fears

Unlike their cousins who can cause quite a stink
Skabbits survive because they're smart and can think
They would make nice pets but are hard to keep
They're awake when boys and girls are asleep

A Chicken
And a Rabbit
… is a Chic-abbit

Ever seen a Chic-abbit …
That hops like a rabbit,
On two skinny legs!
That doesn't lay eggs

It has ears that are floppy
And habits that are sloppy
With white fur on its wings
It wears no jewelry or rings

It has a beak to peck
And will dirty a patio deck
It is cuddly and soft
And sleeps in the loft

Just after it is born
It is raised on corn
But carrots and seeds
Is all it really needs

When at its best
It will just sit on its nest
Even though it doesn't say a word
A Chic-abbit is no ordinary bird

A Rabbit and
A Cat
...is a Cabbit!

A Cabbit is smart
And quick as a dart

It has lots of fur
And loves to purr

With a fury tail
It loves milk in a pail

And a carrot or two
But will never say "BOO"

It sees great at night
With dogs it will fight

It will sleep in your lap
And loves to take a nap

Fond of fish
It will eat from a dish

It is tidy around sand
On its feet it will land

A Lion and A Zebra Is Called A Zeon!

It is often spotted on African grass lands
It lives in large family groups called bands

Its body is white with stripes of black
It has a Lions head and long hair on its back

Grasses and berries are a favorite to eat
And it has a long tail behind its rear seat!

On four thin legs it is quick to run
With other animals it is fun to run!

Although it looks ferocious and scary
The Zeon has many friends on the prairie

The Cheetahs and Wart Hogs are but a few
That know what the Zeon likes to do

Because they enjoy chasing the elephants away
They can play in the water hole for most of the day

A Kangaroo and …
An Antelope
Is a Kangalope!

See the Kangalope run
In the sun it loves to have fun
With horns on its head
It hops, not runs, instead

It can leap over fences and streams
It likes grassy plains, it seems!
Its brown coat has yellow and white
It is hard to see at night!

It can out-hop all who seek it
It certainly is physically fit!
It uses its horns to remove snow
As it seeks to eat the grasses below.

Baby Kangalopes are kept in a pouch
Some say it is really a "kiddy couch"!
In a small herd it is sometimes seen
Their sense of smell is also very keen

For its' home, it does not use a nest
To keep wandering, for safety, is best
Since they only grow to three feet tall
It's a good thing … they're the fastest of all!

A Monkey and Dog … is a *Dogkey*!

A *Dogkey* is rather small …
It is not large at all!

It has a crisp loud bark …
It likes to play in a park!

With a long, thin, curly tail
It can hang from a rail …

Or exercise in a tree!
On three legs it will wee!

On command it will sit.
It has humor and wit!

Its' favorite food is fruit.
It has a black hairy suit

An acrobat on hind legs …
It'll climb a wall of pegs!

It will even return a thrown ball …
Because it's the most fun of all!

A Chicken
And a Duck
... is a Ducken

The amazing Ducken
Struts around "Cluck'n"
If a choice of barn yard or pond
It is the pond of which it's fond

It has no visible ear ...
Yet, it can hear without fear!
The male takes a wife ...
And they mate for life!

With a wide yellow beak it pecks ...
It makes a mess on pool decks
The males' feathers are colorful
In flight ... it is very beautiful

Baby Duckens hatch from eggs
And learn to walk on spindly legs
There is a red comb on its head
From birth, by its' mother, it is led

Rather than just sit on a nest
Swimming is what it does best
Even though it doesn't "Quack"
For beauty, it obviously doesn't lack!

A Buffalo and a Squirrel is called a Squirffalo!

It is most often spotted on American prairies
Constantly grazing for grasses and berries

Unlike its Bison cousin pictured on our nickel
This little four legged animal is a lot more fickle

Although it stands only four feet tall
It can easily jump a five foot wall

With one curved horn on each side of its head
It will lie down at night and use grass for a bed

In winter, it uses its horns to scrape away snow
As it seeks to gobble up the dried grass below.

Patches of grey spot its thick brown hair
It looks quite different from a big brown bear

In a small herd it is sometimes seen
Their sense of smell is also very keen

Squirffaloes also have a long, grey and bushy tail
That bounces behind it scraping the ground like a trail

These cute little fellows appear gentle to girls and boys
But they are too rough to play with, as if they were toys

Gentle and placid for such a cute little beast
To see them in a national park is a visual feast

The Beautiful Butterfly

Beautiful and dainty in size
I couldn't believe my eyes
Shades of Orange, Black and White
It was totally … an awesome sight!

Sitting on a flower petal
It glistened as a jewel in metal
It almost took my breath away
In the breeze it didn't sway

A green caterpillar at first it was
Without a stinger or a buzz
Its' only defense was its' hue
Eating leaves and drops of dew

It even built its own cocoon
And not a moment too soon
Like it was following an order
It struggled to escape its border

A Butterfly it would finally be
And there it was for me to see
Delicate wings allowed it to fly
As it lifted off, I said, "Good-bye"

Blessings of Christmas

This Holiday Season

The Holidays are here again
Stretching our credit cards thin
Holiday music is on the radio
Even strangers are saying hello

Starbucks lines are longer
Retail sales are stronger
People dress in colors brighter
And our wallets become lighter

The weather here is never cold
In San Diego we are never told
What snow and ice are all about
So the children could really shout

As for me, it's just off to the mall
And the traffic jams for cars to stall
I could be waiting a very long time
I think I need a handicapped sign

Trees and homes sparkle with lights
It's a joy to see the Christmas sights
In the harbor they even decorate the boats
They look like very bright …Rose Parade floats

When all of this is said and done
I must not forget my God's only Son
With my family seated at their table
I will honor the baby … born in a stable!

A
Christmas
Tradition

Some say it's all about retail
Yet, we thrive on a Holiday sale
Stores use it to make a big haul
People flock to a crowded mall

Then, on a cold winter's night
When the kids are out of sight
Parents will break out the gifts
And assemble them in shifts

Packages will be wrapped very tight
On display, they're a beautiful sight
For the morning comes fast
And these ribbons won't last

While Dad lights a roaring fire
Children wait with a huge desire
Everyone descends upon the tree
As if these presents were free

With sparkling eyes a'glow
The kids will have lots to show
By the time this ritual is done
We'll all agree it was worth the fun.

Christmas Eve

The Christmas rush finally slows
Naughty or nice ... Santa knows

An evergreen tree glistens bright
Churches assemble in candle light

Sounds of hymns fill the air
Some homes cause people to stare

Thousands of little white lights
Create beautiful seasonal sights

Mall parking lots start to drain
Online sales have eased the strain

Airlines sellout and overbook
Even airports have a holiday look

In Rome thousands assemble for a Pope
Children relish in anticipated hope

Parents wait for the kids to slow
Some things … they shouldn't know

Then when children are finally asleep
And they are in bed without a peep

Grownups go crazy with ribbon and tape
Wrapping gifts of various size and shape

Knowing very well they will not last
Parents assemble and wrap very fast

Setting presents around the tree
They become a magical site to see

Finally, the parents crawl into bed
Knowing now why they were wed

To bring to each child a loving smile
They retreat in private … if only a short while

T'is More Than Christmas!

Christmas Cheer is finally in the air
To brightly lit homes we gladly share

Custom Computerized Cards are sent
Disposable Income is nearly all spent

Shopping Malls stay open longer
So Store Sales can grow stronger

Decorations are always awesome
Seasonal Santas are never lonesome!

Surrounded by Christmas music we enjoy
It makes it easier to find the perfect toy

People parade with a spring in their step
Holiday shops generate energy and pep

For eleven months we save and wait
For our children finally to succinctly state

Their long list of immediate needs
For gifts that outnumber a farmer's seeds

Decoration boxes look a little worn
Some chimney Stockings are torn

Tree Ornaments need new hooks
We love the way … our old house looks!

The Christmas season stimulates kindness
Yet for many Americans there is sadness

And for these we pray their homes be warm
That they might weather the severest storm

We must remember why on Christmas we pray
For the world was changed forever that day

When in a manger, amongst animals, on some hay
Our Lord Jesus was born in a miraculous way!

Season of Light

The Christmas Season is all about lights
Millions of tiny lights create Holiday sights
Lighted homes become fascinating displays
Christmas will be here in just a few days

People are happier and seem to smile
They swamp the malls and shop awhile
Days get shorter as the big day nears
Charge cards are shed instead of tears

Shoppers form an army of substantial size
But if you stay home are you any more wise?
At last, internet sales appear to be soaring
Giving our Santas more time to be snoring

Ships are on parade with lights all around
And if it's a little bit foggy a horn will sound
Stores sparkle beneath bright colored signs
Even the streets have new painted lines

Then, after Thanksgiving, it really starts
The Spirit of Christmas warms our hearts
Our neighbors decorate their private sites
It's the Holiday Season of tiny white lights

Christmas at Starbucks

It's Christmas time at Starbucks again
The holidays are about ready to begin
Store windows are painted in snowy white
Christmas carols create a digital delight

Inside or out, thirsty patrons can stand or sit
But the order line is so long not all will fit
While pillars of merchandise inhibit the line
Extracting more sales from those who dine

Each delicious drink floats its own aroma
To think it all started just north of Tacoma
Who would have thought flavors so strong
Would have been so good with names so long

Some new flavors really seem to attract
A *Christmas Blend* is popular, it's a fact
Holiday drinks made with eggnog and milk
From Tall to Venti, they're as smooth as silk

The shoppe is crowded with caffeine seekers
Seven days a week there are lots of believers
There is even a place for a wireless lap top
To work and sip … to the very last drop

People enjoy the comfortable holiday setting
Sales will increase, stockholders are betting
With the Spirit of the Holidays alive and well
No wonder so many … think Starbucks is swell

The Magic of Santa

Each year on Christmas eve night
From out of the northern light
There appears a mysterious sight
And a white bearded man takes flight

Tucked warmly in a radical red sled
Eight tiny reindeer by GPS are led
So that toys crafted from his work shed
Be exchanged for milk and sweetbread

The plump little dude waves and smiles
Confident he can last the necessary miles
There are toys made in countless styles
And hi-tech gadgets with digital dials

Soon, millions of excited children will see
Neatly placed around a Christmas tree
Bright colored gifts that are left there to be
Arranged by him as if they were free

Once every year Santa visits the kids
Landing on roof tops in a sled with skids
Luckily, it's not about politics or union bids
Or aluminum cans with pull-top lids

Even those who don't believe will swear
Christmas morning finds kindness in the air
Because it's a magical time for all who care
Especially the kids who know … Santa was there!

Essays

CHANGE: It's more than just a few coins in a pocket!

CHANGE can be quantified
And probably should be verified
It can be given or received
But don't be deceived

It might be a thing of the past
Nothing ever seems to last
It's not used with plastic,
Which is not exactly drastic.

Men use CHANGE as a toy
Most started fondling coins as a boy
Coins of CHANGE are fun to collect
I had a collection, I recollect!

But Girls are a different breed
CHANGE to them expresses a need
To CHANGE clothes is sometimes a must
Not enough outfits can be a real bust

So, clothes are changed as much as most
Wearing dirty socks is nothing to boast
We all like the smell of new and clean
The concept of CHANGE can be quite keen

Politicians are always talking CHANGE too
As a gimmick to push legislation through
But voters like to CHANGE them as well
To answer the roll call voting bell!

How Much is Luck!

My parents happened to be nice
But, isn't it just a roll of the dice?
No one actually has a voice!
Who gets a choice?

Even their personalities rubbed off
Mom was tough, but Dad was soft
Albeit, they were rather small
I, too, am not very tall

But they were very athletic and trim
And I too, grew up looking rather slim
My parents are both gone now
But, should they have taken a bow!

At least my family tree is tall
I even hang it on a wall
Dating back to AD 805
What a time to be alive!

OK, so my genes are the same
It's all a part of life's little game
Looking back on it, I had some luck
Hey … some kids, I know, got stuck.!

A Friend

It's nice to have a very special friend
Someone to talk to … at the day's end
But it has to be more than that
After all, just about anyone can chat
                    No sir, a friend is very unique
                Someone, who into your mind can peek
                    Who knows what you like
                Whether it be tennis or riding a bike
Be it a little girl or neighborhood boy
When young, a friend can share life's joy
Someone to shoot baskets with at home
A trusted buddy with whom to explore and roam
                    A friend knows how you feel
                To help you stay on an even keel
                Who laughs when things are funny
                Who says, "It's not about the money"
When the chips are down
They encourage a smile and not a frown
They know just what to say
It's easy to love their wonderful way
                    A friend enjoys the things you do
                It's like one mind instead of two
                Whether it a movie or game to play
                They enhance each and every day
They lend a hand when there is need
For good ideas … they can plant a seed
When in life you're ever sick or ill
They have a knack to pump up your will

Thanksgiving:
Yesterday and Today

Thanksgiving is gratitude
It takes a humble attitude
Knowing we can't do it all
On God we call

As the tale is told
The Pilgrims were bold
Life was very tough
The winter was rough

Disease became a thorn
Indians gave them corn
A village was saved
And in God they behaved

Together they gathered
And with Indians feathered
To a banquet they came
With hearts the same

So, Lord, before we begain
Thank You once again
Since we ask of You
To Bless what we do

And then I met
a Blind Man

I have a good life
Although not a wife
My life is fine
I enjoy good food and wine

> At Starbucks a coffee I enjoy
> For me, poetry is a toy
> I write whatever I hear and see
> Most of my stuff is all about me!

Fiction thrillers I love to read
On a Kindle my mind I feed
Even a Netflix movie I like
My hip won't let me ride a bike

> Tennis and Pickleball I play a lot
> Even a new paddle I just bought
> To rush the net and volley
> Excites like a San Francisco Trolley

I've seen Sequoia and Redwood trees
In a glass jar I've captured honey bees
I've seen the wonders of Yellowstone
And old age I've tried to postpone

> And then one day I met a blind man
> Forcing me to recall how lucky I am!
> As I approached I put my hand in his
> And then pondered his mind to quiz

Oh, how I wish I could say the words,
"Rise, nice man, and see that flock of birds!"
Instead, his warm smile melted my heart
And encouraged a conversation to start!

Valentine's Day
... All year Long!

The best 24 hours in February is the 14th Day
It's all about Valentines and what they say!
Cute little poems of love are tucked inside
To someone special we open our hearts wide!

Remember as a child a book of cutouts
The purpose was clear so as to leave no doubts!
Some kids got a lot ... and some got a few
To that special friend they said ... "I love you"!

To know how it started really doesn't matter
But eat all the candy and your brain will scatter!
That's probably why flowers are such a wise choice
It's an expression of love in a very loud voice!

Wouldn't it be wonderful if it lasted all year
Such feelings of tenderness we all want to hear!
For two people in love, it's a day to appreciate
All that is needed ... is for each one to communicate!

On Being a Mom

Only by Godly design
Could it work perfectly fine
Regardless of where
Only a mom can bear

Sickness arrives within days
Sadly, it's only a mom that pays
Slowly her belly will swell
Only after birth is she well

And then the hard part starts
Taking care of all baby's parts
Like feedings around the clock
Making sure there's a clean sock

Giving and giving of time and self
Regardless of position or wealth
With unselfish love and care
Beyond what a man would bear

God fits moms for many hats
Even more than a book about cats
A mom's job is just never done
But in the end she will have won

However tough the job might seem
A mom's heart will always beam
Having been the only one to bear
Her right to our love is always there

Time is to Life …
Like Acts in a Play!

Consider just how fast
Today becomes the past!
Like the blink of an eye
"Hello" fades … just before bye!

Time is allocated to all each day
In a very precise, calculated way!
Regardless of stature or class
All must use the same hour-glass!

Why then, do some days seem long?
Must we all be physically strong?
Why do many days blend into one?
Are a few days shorter than some?

Although man inserted an extra day
And yes, Leap Year is here to stay …
Nature's clock continues to click
As a miracle, it is rather slick!

The sun rises because earth spins
That way …at least everybody wins!
Day becomes Night followed by Day
I guess God thought it best that way!

What counts is how our time is spent
Since from God our lives are lent!
Like a play, life has a number of days certain
Before we are called for our final curtain!

Things In Life That Are Free

Have you ever noticed that
　　many good things in life are free?
There are sunsets and rainbows
　　and snowflakes to see.
There are chirping birds
　　and sounds made by crickets.
For these, thank God,
　　we do not need to buy tickets!
On a clear night, it's fun to spot and wish
　　upon the first star.
Shining from millions of miles away,
　　its' light travels incredibly far.
An awesome sight is to see a perfectly full moon
　　rise in the east.
From a quarter of a million miles,
　　it becomes a visionary feast!
To see a flock of birds you only need a handful of seed.
To find the North Star,
　　locate the Big Dipper and follow its lead.
Unfortunately, not all of nature's wonders
　　are we able to behold.
They're so many beautiful scenes on earth,
　　they can't all be told!
Yet, in addition to these,
　　there are things people CAN DO for free.
They can reflect their own happiness,
　　by their smile, we can see!
A kind word of encouragement,
　　or a helping hand at the right time,
Can be more valuable
　　than reaching in a pocket and lending a dime!

Dove Love

In the Spring of 2014
    Just right of the front door
Two doves had started a nest
    For a family of three or more
Out of sticks, grass and fuzz
    More than a week it took
Between the rain gutter and eve
    You really had to look

Alternating one at a time
    Each parent took a turn
Adding comfort to the nest
    Now, there is something we can learn
While one sat on the nest
    Motionless, not wanting to be found
A few feet away in a lemon tree
    Was heard a soft cooing sound

It's not very often you observe
    a sleek, gray Mourning Dove
With its look-a-like partner
    Demonstrating a Dove's Love
Selected by Noah
    To reconnoiter dry land
The mourning dove's neck
    Has a thin black band

Unique and special
    Are the bird's patterns and sounds
From quick darting flight,
    To the cooing lament of a dove in love!

Pickleball ... What?

Take a plastic ball and punch it with holes
Ware a pair of shoes with rubber soles
Color the sphere with bright yellow paint
Learn to hit it softly and you'll be a saint

Separate sides by a 34 inch net
Play to eleven instead of a set
Use a court only twenty by twenty-two
It will be easier for doubles to do

Use a small paddle without any strings
The plastic ball will sound like it pings
It can be played indoors or out
It's so fun you'll want to shout

Men and women both love this game
They play it for fun and not for fame
Play starts with an underhand serve
Unlike tennis it doesn't take a lot of nerve

Just stay out of the kitchen unless it bounces
The slippery little ball only weighs a few ounces
Since a lot of the game takes place in the kitchen!
Develop a good dink and ... you'll do just bitch'n!

Biblical and Religious

A Baby in a Basket
(Exodus: Ch. 1-14)

A story is told how Egypt held a Hebrew people captive
That was propagating too quickly, for Pharaoh to let live
So an order went out to drown Jewish boys in the Nile
But to only let female babies live was not the Jewish style

Soon, a baby boy was found among some river reeds
Concealed in a basket, he'd been born with Jewish seeds
Little did Pharaoh's daughter know, it was all God's plan
For Moses to lead a Jewish exodus from her father's land

But other things had to take place for everything to work
Moses killed an Egyptian slave driver, for being a jerk
He even hid in a foreign village, to escape being caught
Only to meet God's burning bush, so he could be taught

Moses had some doubts about the plan God conceived
But after a snake turned back into a staff, he felt relieved
Maybe Pharaoh would finally agree to let His people go
Until God had sent ten plagues, Pharaoh had said, "No"

Now, Moses had a speech problem and could hardly talk
Although he was a great man, selected from Jewish stalk
His older brother Aaron, was Moses's authoritative voice
He was Moses only hope, and Aaron was God's choice

Finally, Pharaoh said he had enough, and let them leave
But he lied to Moses, and had something up his sleeve
The treacherous Egyptian ruler angered God yet again
And God made sure that the Pharaoh did not win

God let it be known only to the Jewish people His plan
How he would save His people all over Pharaoh's land
So God passed over the Jews with blood above their door
But every first born Egyptian would lay dead on the floor

When the Jews escaped into the desert that first night
Moses confidently told them not to fear an Egyptian fight
Even though Pharaoh sent his army to bring them back
God parted the Red Sea and drown their army …
                                   before they could attack!

At the END … of the Pew

"And the last shall be first"
So say those with a Biblical thirst
But does that mean first "in"… or first "out"?
For such as this, there must be … no doubt!

Consider the seat at the end of the pew
Occupied weekly by the same very few!
They will even stand up to let you through
When moving center … is better to do!

It's like they actually claim that end place
Or do they tithe more for the title to that space?
They always seem to be … the first one there!
Is this spot too important for them to share?

Jesus said there would be a narrow gate!
But not for those who come in late!
Sometimes they are reluctant to stand
Before you can find a seat and land!

Is it all about maintaining total control?
So permission is theirs to ultimately dole!
Does being "first" really mean so much
As to stake a claim … on an end seat, as such!

Daily Strength

Oh, Jesus, Prince of Peace
My life from you I gladly lease
You forgive me although I sin
By faith in You, I'm destined to win

For every up there appears a down
Yet, with Jesus I need not frown
By faith I have taken a stand
For Daily Strength I trust your hand

As I 'waken each and every day
I recall you taught me how to pray
To show respect and give thanks to you
For opportunity in life and all you do

Most days are sunny, some have rain
But your love for me will never wan
Each morning I reach with outstretched hand
And try to follow Jesus … footprints in the sand

God is Real

So many times in life
God's omnipotence is real
In just the right way
His presence I can feel
                While driving a car
                When danger appears
                So imminently close
                His hands I can feel
                            When in need of help
                            No place to turn
                            Out of nowhere
                            His solution I can feel
        When hiking a Sierra trail
        Tired and dry
        Dehydrated and hot
        His cool breeze I can feel
When asked about life
By a child bright and smart
Caught off guard
His answer I (could) feel
                When in the wrong
                Unaware of my faults
                Discouraged and mad
                His forgiveness I can feel
                            When happy and glad
                            Counting my blessings
                            Enjoying a precious moment
                            His love I can feel

The Easter Story …
He Lives!

Jesus died for you and for Me
Even though I wasn't there to see
They tortured him first
To fulfill prophecy he thirst

They denied him a fair trial
Fed him the customary bile
Stabbed him with a spear
Yet, He died without fear

Then, just as he had foretold
He walked about very bold
Thomas witnessed his hands
And the Easter story … spread to other lands

Inspired by God

Biblical stories are there to be found
Inspired by God … the Bible is sound
Accordingly, they are considered the truth
From Eve and Adam to David and Ruth

There are love stories and tales of strength
There are short stories and some of greater length
You'll find gardens, and floods, and even animals
Just like donkeys, sheep, lions, and camels

The Biblical testaments from the old to the new
Are not about the many, but more about the few
One passage describes a very narrow gate
Another encourages faith, before it's too late

It's amazing, the history within its pages
The Bible unfolds in humanitarian stages
Parables by Jesus offer soothing refrain
Using human characters to touch our brain

There are miracles and works difficult to believe
To sacrifice one's son is impossible to conceive
Yet, that's exactly the end God had in mind
Hoping all mankind … His Son, they would find

Since none of us were actually there
We trust the writers to be honest and fair
Considering we are all sinful and lost
Thanks be to God … His Son paid the cost!

John: Chapter 4 - Jocob's Well ... and a Big Bronze Bell

What if there had been a Big Bronze Bell
To announce visitors at Jacob's Well!
How many years would have to pass?
How much sand through an hour glass?
Would it have been in a state of needed repair?
Located in the Samarian town of Sychar there
Many generations would pass 'til the historic day
When God's Son, Jesus, would pass this way!
Fortunately, the Gospel of John records this event
Although there's no mention of a pitched tent
You'd expect Jesus to find some form of shade
During the few hours He must have stayed!
As was custom, Jews didn't talk to Samarians there
But Jesus used the occasion for His Light to bear
He asked a Samarian woman to help Him with a drink
Surprised, she probably didn't know what to think!
Confused, she reminded him that he was a male Jew
Obviously, she wasn't aware of what His disciples knew
The concept of Living Water to her was shockingly new!
How could she have known it was absolutely true!
After all, there was no Big Bronze Bell to sound
She couldn't herald the Man at the well she'd found
Furthermore, Jesus was abstract, yet simple, in his speech
As was His style whenever a point He wanted to teach
The concept of Living Water was made quite clear
Accept Jesus as Christ and He will forever stay near
Like the Samarian woman at the site of Jacob's Well
We all need to listen ... for a "Big Bronze Bell"

Luke: Chapter 18
A Blind Beggar Sees

On a dusty, dirt road outside Jericho
Where Jesus and his disciples were soon to go
A sightless beggar patiently sat
And inquired, "What commotion is that?"
When told it was Jesus passing bye
He exhaled in relief and heaved a sigh
Aware of the urgency, he formed a plan
To somehow attract God's miraculous man

"Jesus, Son of David, " he blurted out
Offended, Jesus friends said, "Please don't shout!"
But louder still, he repeated his call
And he yelled even louder above them all!
After all, his life depended on Jesus to be
The Son of God, so they too might see
If Jesus were to perform a miracle again
The Beggars new life right here would begin

As planned, Jesus looked toward the noise
Knowing it was not a little boy with his toys
Jesus asked, "What can I do for you?"
And the Beggar replied," I want to see too!"
 Instantly, the man received his lost sight.
And his whole world was suddenly bright
It was the Beggar's faith Jesus had felt
And before our Lord … the Beggar knelt
Such happiness that day was witnessed by many
Who watched a Beggar without even a penny
Take up his mat and follow Jesus to town
Exclaiming Jesus, the Christ, to all whom he found

Miracles ...
For Our Faith

Jesus performed many miraculous things
Because we, like disciples, are sinful human beings
Lucky for us, however, some of these were recorded
But the price HE paid ... we could not have afforded

HE healed the lame and HE cured the sick
And HE did all of this ... without faking a trick
At a wedding HE turned water into wine
On a lake HE walked on the water just fine!

HE told strangers HE met, where they had been
(John the Baptist claimed Jesus walked without sin)
A Roman Centurion approached HIM for a favor
Jesus healed his servant by faith ... not labor!

One day as HE passed through the gate at Nain
HE observed a small coffin and a mother in pain
Having compassion HE said to her, "Don't cry"
And the boy came to life ... before she could say, "Why?"

On one occasion in a boat with His disciples Jesus slept
But a storm came upon the lake where the boat was kept
So Jesus was awakened and calmed the waters and wind
But HIS greatest miracle was forgiving us who sinned!

Of
Love
And
God

If Love abounds within
In God it must begin
For God is perfect Love
Here on earth and above

God gave Man an example
After Eve bit into an apple
Knowing Man was about to fall
God sent Jesus for one and all

God's wish is an abundant life
His Love combats daily strife
It can feed a huge healthy heart
Necessary for each day to start

God's Love sustains the weary
Just as time heals the teary
His Love encourages hope
And washes sin better than soap

"One More Day"
... a prayer

Lord, my life has one more day
So, today I ask you lead the way
Although, at times, I've walked alone
I'm grateful, Lord, my path you've shown

I'm told you once on water walked
To crowds in parables you sincerely talked
As much as I would've loved to hear
I'm glad this day my life you'll steer

In the twilight of my life it's getting late
My focus now is toward a narrow gate
And since my body's handicapped from age
I turn to you, Lord, for my final stage!

Quiet Time

In a moment of absolute quiet
I feel the beat of my heart
My breathing is slowed
I don't know how to start

I open my eyes and smile
It feels good to be in prayer
Doused in God's love
It feels good to be there

I give thanks to be alive
To be His baptized child
I feel secure in my faith
In a world gone wild

I thank His forgiveness
I acknowledge His omnipotence
In quiet and soothing comfort
God's presence gives confidence

My petitions are heard
They always are
God already knows my heart
From His love … I wander not far

"Sorry, but I will Pray for You!"

There are times we confess
    Our troubles to another
Only to be told "Sorry,
        "But I will pray for my 'brother'"!
Hmmm, is that your final offer?
    When it's really time I seek
It's not dollars I ask or want
        It's about my faucet with a leak!

I can see how people are afraid
    Their time to commit
When it is so much easier
        Their prayer to submit!
Is this what our Lord meant
    When he taught us to pray
In his sermon on a mount
        When he showed us the way

When our "Ox cart" is in a ditch
    Should we expect only prayer
From our friends who believe
        But want not to help there
Sure, we need all the prayer
    But what about lending a hand?
A concert would get poor reviews
        Without a lead singer in the band!

John: Chapter 2

Wedding Wine Miracle

The town of Cana was in the state of Galilee
It was by invitation the very place to **be**
It was here Jesus performed a miracle
So (the Disciples) in attendance "**might see**"

It happened at a Jewish wedding feast
As planned, only a few people would **know**
CNN, CBS, FOX and C-SPAN were not
And there was no morning radio talk **show!**

However, as happens at parties like these
The wine runs out way too **soon!**
To order more would take too long
It might not arrive 'til tomorrow **noon!**

Now enter Mary, Jesus Mother (as told by "John")
For She had noticed the problem **too**
Wisely, She calmly advised the Banquet Master
"Listen to Jesus, He will tell you … what to **do**"

As the Bridegroom stood dumbfounded and watched
Jesus instinctively questioned His Mother's **request**
He was heard to say, "My time had not yet come"
But His Mother obviously knew what was **best!**

Turning to the Banquet Master reluctantly
Jesus pointed the servants to a water jar of **stone**
"Take six of these to the well and fill them with water"
(But at thirty gallons each, one could not carry it **alone!)**

This done, Jesus once again gave instructions
"Draw out a cup for the Banquet Master to **taste"**
Amazingly, the water turned to an award winning wine!
"This", the Master said, "you certainly shouldn't **waste"**

Until then, only His Mother and the servants knew
What had miraculously taken **place**
Yet the result was gladly appreciated
By the look … on the Bridegroom's **face!**

The New Testament

It is a collection of only 27 books*
But none describe Jesus' looks
Its purpose seems to fulfill
Prophets ... shouting God's will
                              The Gospels number only four
                              Yet they set the scene for more
                        They introduce us to Peter and John
                        And ten others the story is based on
It tells us John the Baptist walked about
"I am not Him," he would shout
He was Jesus cousin as it turned out
Used by God to introduce Him throughout
                              To embellish some major facts
                        Inserted next ... is the book of Acts
                        Introduced herein is a Roman Jew
                  Of which there must have been only a few
On a road to Damascus he was blinded by light
Until God himself gave him his sight
Paul was the Billy Graham of his day
Teaching us ... from the cross not to stray
                        Many of his letters are printed next
                        In a series of books they form a text
                  Some to individuals ... some to a church
                  Lost as sea he was rescued by a search
The last book describes a futuristic dream
Insuring hope to mankind ... it would seem
It also describes a great battle and war ...
Assuring us ... Jesus' return ... appears to be in store

*According to Protestant versions

Lord …

The

Question

Is …

Each morning I 'wake
Your love I take
To help each day
You Light my way

You enable me to hear
You remove all my fear
You allow me to see
You insist it be WE … not me

The Question I then must ask
Since in Your love I bask
Like Zacchaeus in the tree
What do YOU … ask of ME!

The Tower of Babel

Gen. 11:1-8

The waters receded after the Great Flood
Noah's family began to spread and multiply
Pairs of animals left the Ark and prospered
Vegetation was in abundant supply

Harmony reigned all over the earth
Only one language had to be spoken
One common tongue among all people
And this, God decided, had to be broken

Understanding one language was a nice advantage
It was easy to get things done
Meanwhile, building materials also changed
Sun dried Bricks and tar replaced stone … for one

Brick walls could be built higher than stone
One upon the other amounted to less weight
So Noah's descendants decided to build a tower
A monument to their industrious state

Naturally, God was aware and watching
And He didn't like what He saw
So God dispersed the people all over the earth
And the idea of a tower started to thaw

Different languages began to be spoken
Communication immediately became confusing
 Thus, the name, "The Tower of Babel"
As if it were … "of man's own choosing"

Worry Not … Today
Tomorrow is Tomorrow

Lord … it's about *TOMORROW*!
Yet, Today, if I hold your hand …
With You at my side …
On my feet I know I'll land

I trust Your absolute love
You always comfort me
Tomorrow is Tomorrow
Today I need to walk with Thee

Today You strengthen me
I sense Your omnipotent power
Doubt plays no part of Today
You accompany me … each hour

My life is full and wonderful
I am loved by family and friends
My mind is sharp and healthy
I know how everything ends

Today is Today!
Like Today, Tomorrow you'll be there
Christ, my Lord, is my assurance
I worry not Today … nor have a care

FOR ME!

If I had been there too
I wonder what I would do
I doubt that I would believe
A Miracle so difficult to conceive!

They said in a Roman court Jesus was tried
Instead, they led him to Pontius Pilot and lied
(Like Pilot, would I have just washed my hands!)
As His Blood dripped from sharp, thorny bands!

So many people wanted Him dead
(I should have worshipped Him instead!)
Through the mob it would be hard to see
As Jesus was savagely beaten ... *for ME*

To the Romans He was danger
To the Jews Jesus was a stranger
(Would I have believed and been His friend?)
He promised I'd know before the end

Dragging a wooden cross with all His might
I'm sure I would've wept at such a sight
(Would I have helped, or left Him be?)
That's the question important to me!

In a stranger's tomb Jesus was laid
For my life he sacrificed and paid
He promised eternity my soul to be
Jesus was crucified ... *for ME*

I doubted the truth He said
So to the grave I must be led
But a guard already told the other pair
It was true ... Jesus body was not there!

And now, *for ME*, He's always there
To listen to my every prayer
He knows my mind as well as my heart
It's about time by faith I start

I shall ask His forgiveness indeed
For I am the one so much in need
Jesus is definitely alive, now I see
He actually defeated death ... *for ME*

 At last I do know why
 For ME Jesus had to die
The tomb is empty, that I can see
Jesus is ALIVE ... *for ME*

Acknowledgments

This collection of poems reflects on many different subjects that have taken place during my, (up until publication time) 74 years of life. Even though most of the poems in this volume, like Volume I, were written in the last ten years, they relate to many events, occurrences, and memories from earlier in my life. As I grow closer to the day I pass on to eternity, I find myself reflecting on years passed. I still talk to my parents and grandparents in my mind from time to time. They were the closest to me and probably influenced my personality, my likes, and my dislikes the most. My father taught me how to shoot and clean a shotgun and hold a small grouping with a rifle, hunt doves, make a camp fire, set up a tent, and bait a fish hook on a trout line. He showed me how to use wood working tools to make a bedroom lamp-table, how to take care of a car under the hood, how to mow the lawn, and how to sketch and draw shapes in perspective. He also was the first one to teach me how to make the best scrambled eggs and "hot" Shredded Wheat cereal with butter and salt. He showed me how to diagram word problems in my ninth grade Algebra book and how to use his "Slide Rule" and "Drafting Machine." And he was the one who had to teach me how to drive a car, Mom's 56 T-Bird! He was an amazing man, and the son of another intelligent and successful man, my grandfather. It is to these people, my parents, and grandparents, who inspired me to become the best dad and grandfather I could be that I must acknowledge my success in writing these poems.

18191186R00084

Made in the USA
San Bernardino, CA
03 January 2015